to Debra

QUINTET FOR PIANO AND STRINGS

I. Annunciation

*equivalent in value to an eighth note

RICHARD DANIELPOUR

QUINTET FOR PIANO AND STRINGS

(2 Violins, Viola, Cello, and Piano)

AMP-8060

First Printing: December 1993

Associated Music Publishers, Inc.

Distributed by

Hal Leonard Publishing Corporation
7777 West Bluemound Road P.O. Box 13819 Milwaukee, WI 53213

Program Note

My Piano Quintet was begun in June of 1988 in New York and was completed that September in Bellagio, Italy.

The movement titles, Annunciation, Atonement, and Apotheosis are not meant to imply a hidden programmatic agenda but rather suggest the nature and profile of the individual movements and the arc of the composition as a whole. The second movement, Atonement ('At-one-ment') is an *adagio* that emphasizes the lyrical, conversational, and coloristic aspects of the work. It is the heart and core of the composition—not only due to its central placement but more importantly because it is dramatically and structurally the major pivotal point of the work. By contrast, the fast outer movements (with their extroverted rhythmic energies) deal with a sense of conflict in need of transformation (movement I) and the result of that transformation (movement III).

The composition of this work was greatly facilitated by Fellowship Residencies at the MacDowell Colony, the Virginia Center for the Creative Arts, and the Rockefeller Foundation at Bellagio, Italy.

—RICHARD DANIELPOUR, 1989

Quintet for Piano and Strings was commissioned by the Chamber Music Society of Lincoln Center. The premiere performance was given on January 6, 1989 by the Emerson String Quartet and Ken Noda, piano at Lincoln Center in New York City.

duration: ca. 28 minutes

recording: Koch International Classics 3-7100-2,
The Chamber Music Society of Lincoln Center:
Christopher O'Riley, piano
Ida Kavafian, Carmit Zori, violins
Scott St. John, viola, Fred Sherry, cello

(Lo stesso tempo ♩ = ca. 116-120)

(Lo stesso tempo ♩ = ca. 116-120)

Ped. as needed

Senza Ped.

*All grace notes should be played on the beat.

14

*ossia: use damper pedal

*Sost. ped.

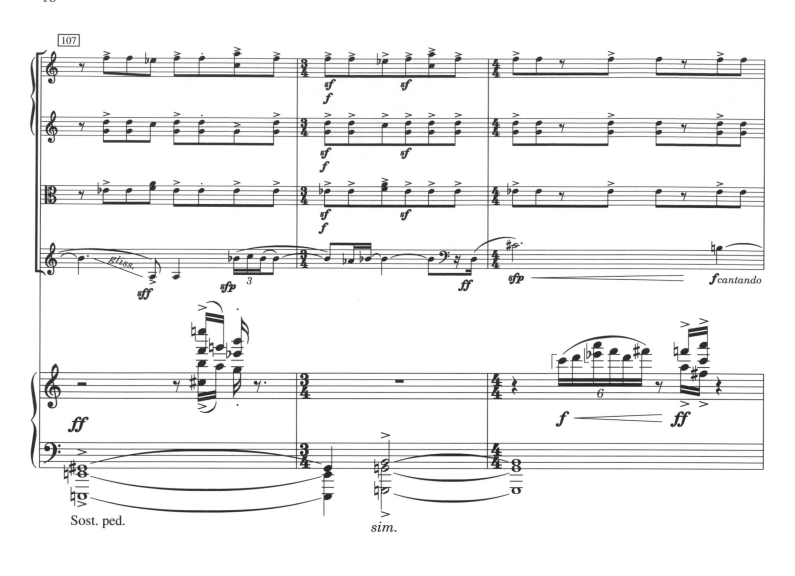

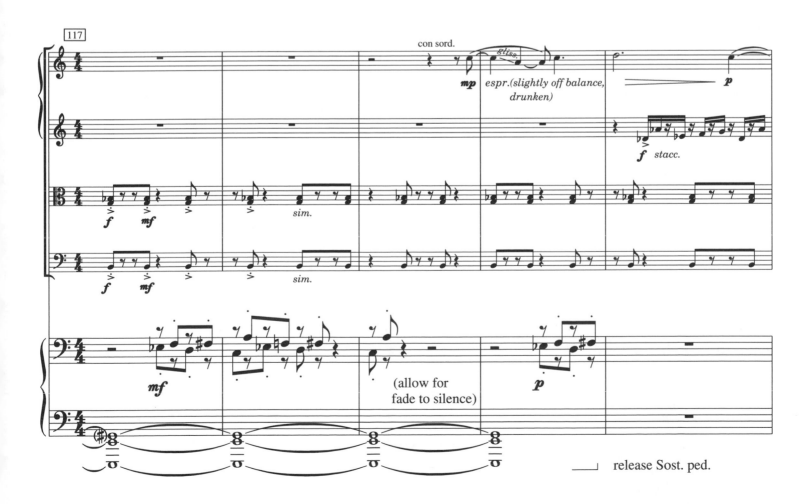

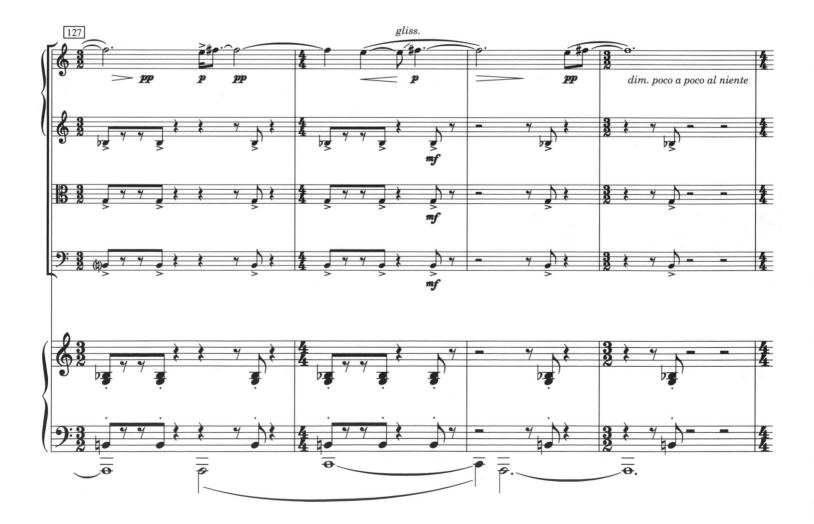

= ca. 116 (Pochiss. meno mosso
con più risoluto)

= ca. 116 (Pochiss. meno mosso
con più risoluto)

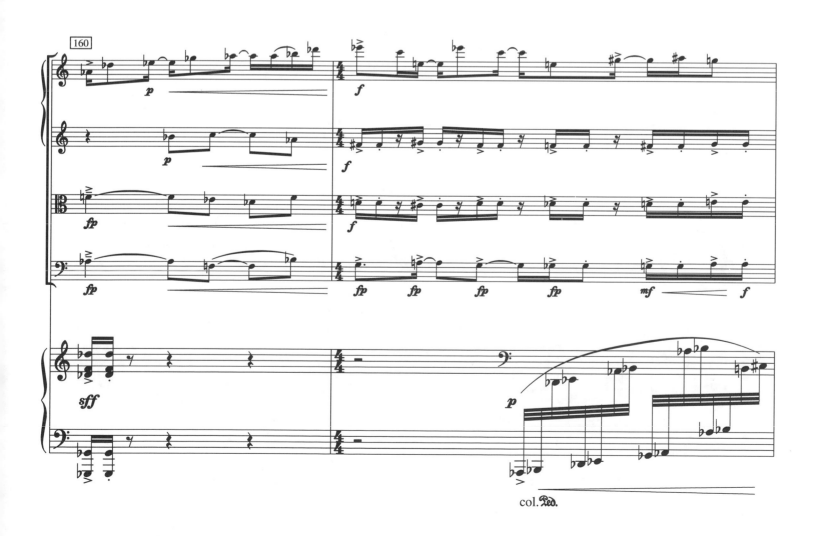

col. Ped.

senza Ped.

♩ = ca. 112 - 116 (Lo stesso tempo)
Cantando e semplice

♩ = ca. 112 - 116 (Lo stesso tempo)
Cantando e semplice

Con energia ♩ = ca. 116
(come prima)

II. Atonement

Lento e triste ♩ = ca. 72

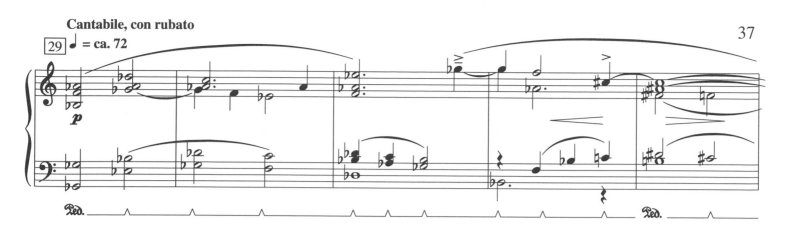

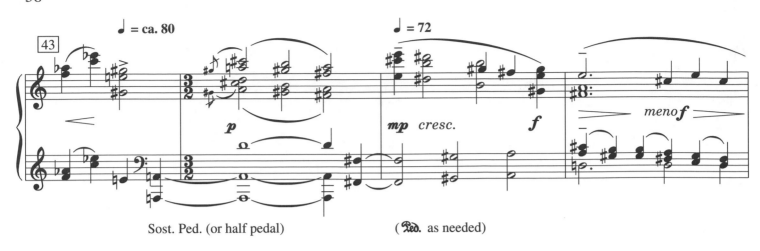

Sost. Ped. (or half pedal)   (Ped. as needed)

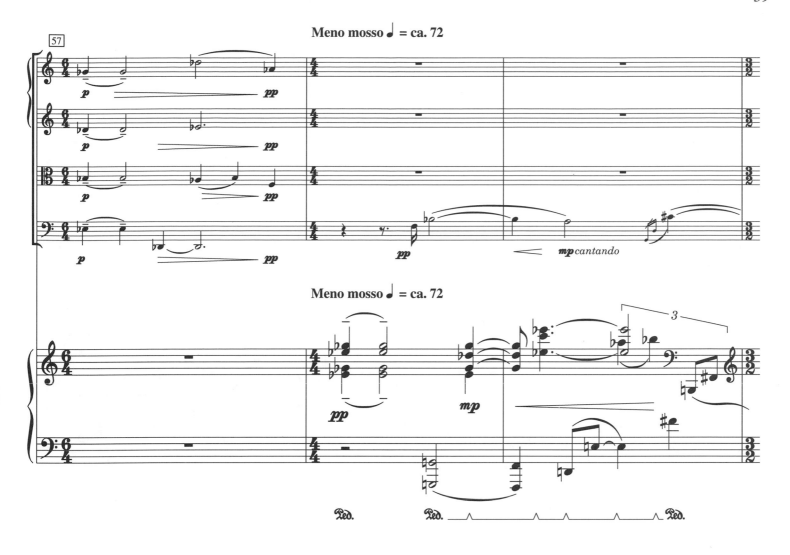

40

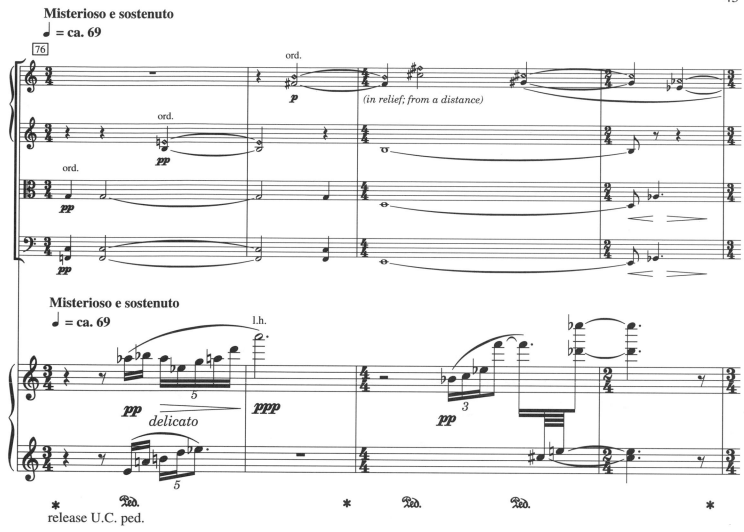

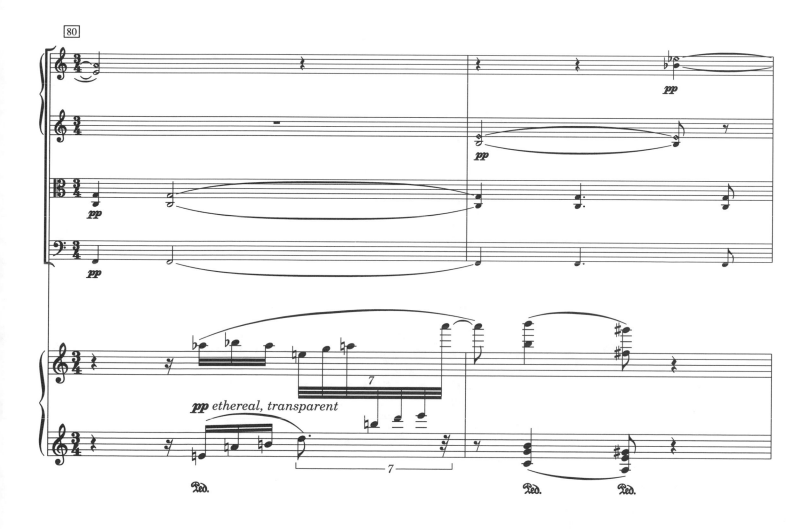

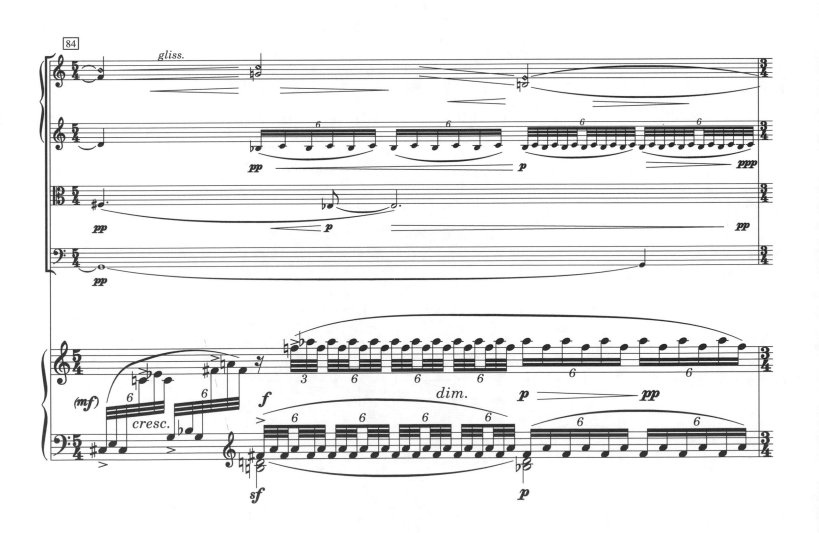

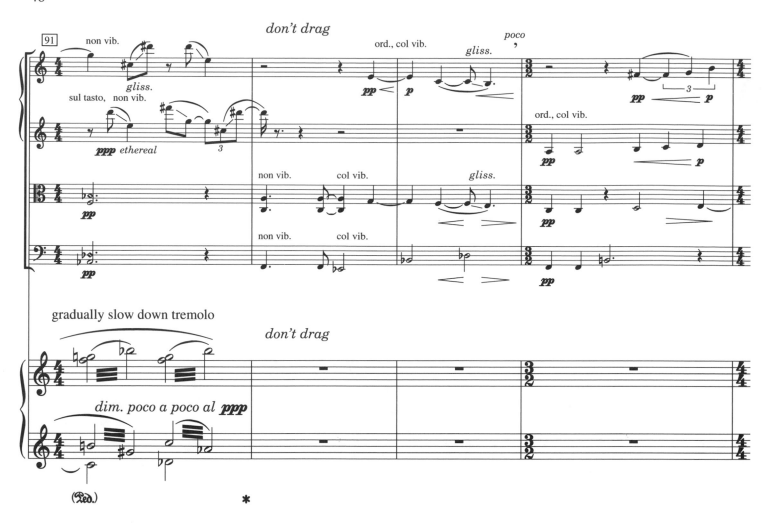

* before the beat

Sost. ped.

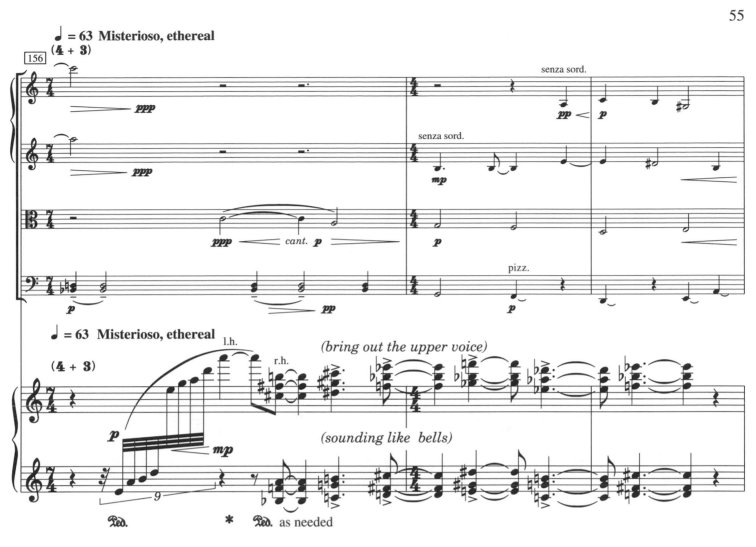

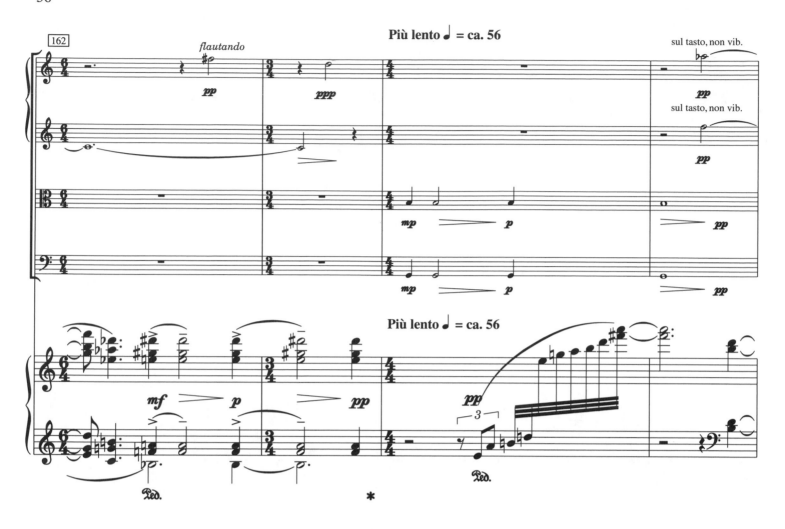

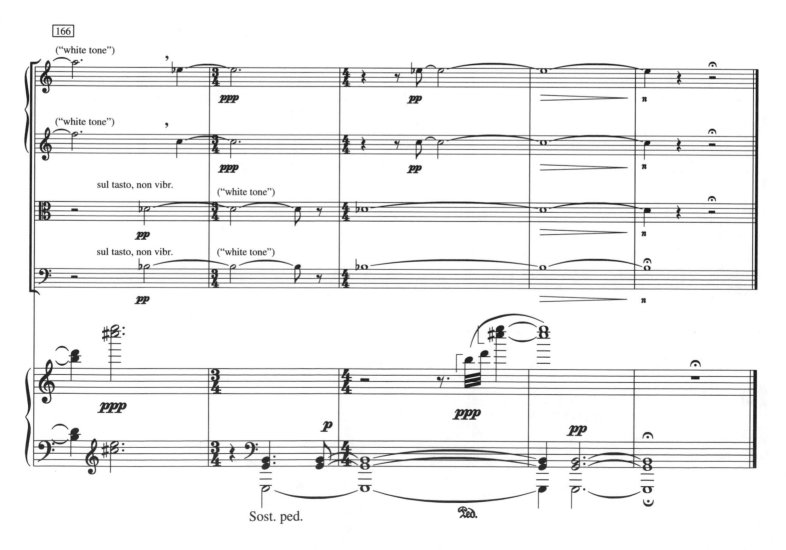

III. Apotheosis

poco rall.

poco rall.

Meno mosso, più grazioso

$\downarrow$ = ca. 52 - 54

(2 + 3)

Meno mosso, più grazioso

$\downarrow$ = ca. 52 - 54

(2 + 3)

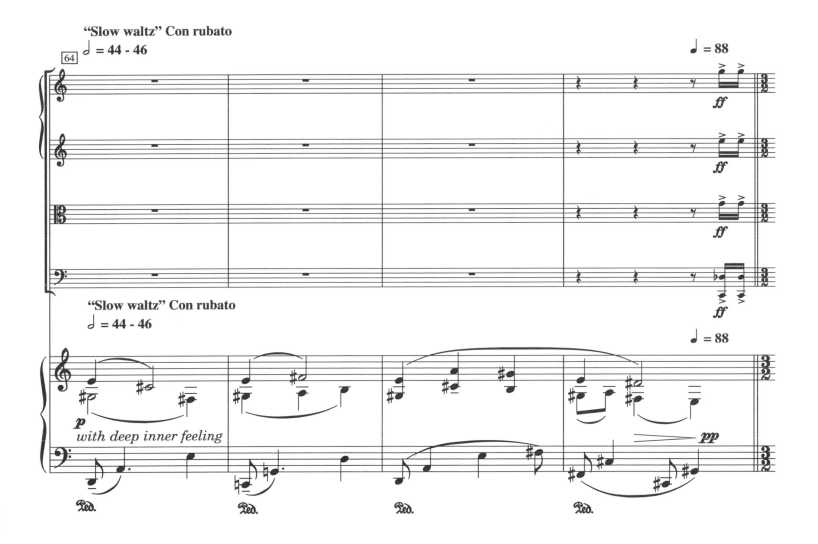

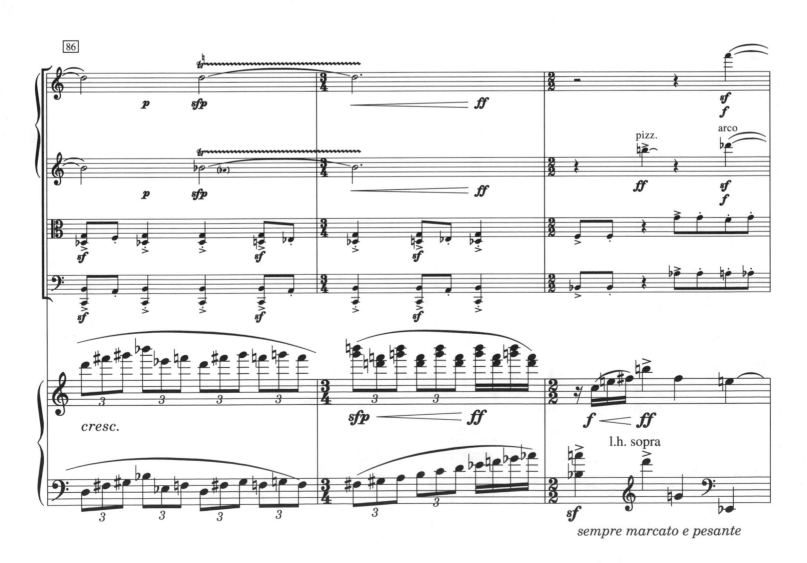

sempre marcato e pesante

*The player may omit the first note if there is not enough time to change from arco to pizz.

bring out the left hand

(𝄟 as needed)

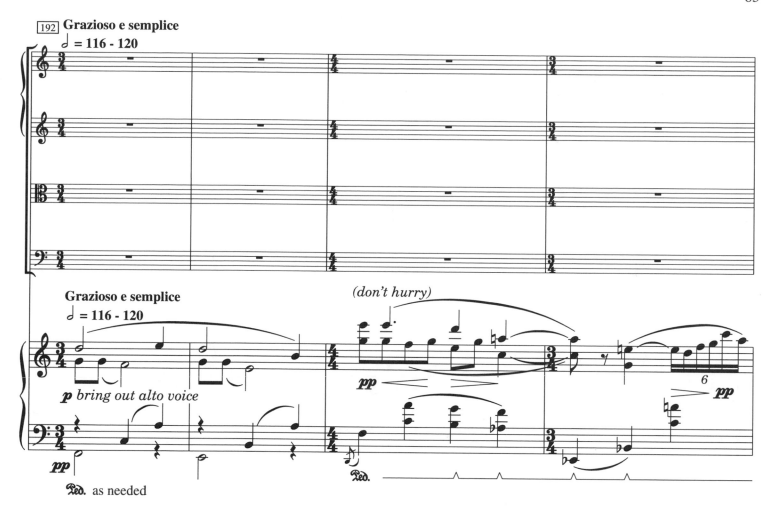

211 **Con energia (bright, rhythmic)**

Con energia (bright, rhythmic)

Ped. as needed   *

(Ped. as needed)

Ped. as needed

Ped. *

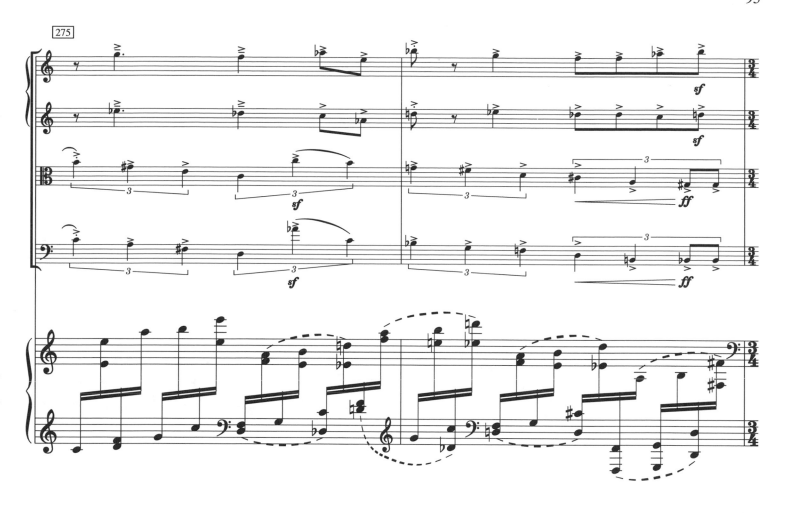

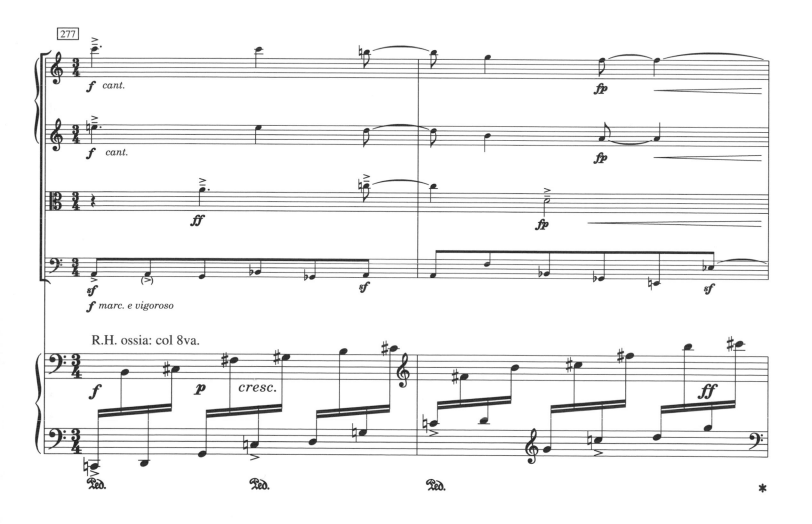